GOD'S LOVE IS LIKE...

RICK CARROL

WESTBOW
PRESS®
A DIVISION OF THOMAS NELSON
& ZONDERVAN

Copyright © 2022 Rick Carrol.

All rights reserved. No part of this book may be used or reproduced by any means, graphic, electronic, or mechanical, including photocopying, recording, taping or by any information storage retrieval system without the written permission of the author except in the case of brief quotations embodied in critical articles and reviews.

This book is a work of non-fiction. Unless otherwise noted, the author and the publisher make no explicit guarantees as to the accuracy of the information contained in this book and in some cases, names of people and places have been altered to protect their privacy.

WestBow Press books may be ordered through booksellers or by contacting:

WestBow Press
A Division of Thomas Nelson & Zondervan
1663 Liberty Drive
Bloomington, IN 47403
www.westbowpress.com
844-714-3454

Because of the dynamic nature of the Internet, any web addresses or links contained in this book may have changed since publication and may no longer be valid. The views expressed in this work are solely those of the author and do not necessarily reflect the views of the publisher, and the publisher hereby disclaims any responsibility for them.

Any people depicted in stock imagery provided by Getty Images are models, and such images are being used for illustrative purposes only. Certain stock imagery © Getty Images.

Scripture quotations marked (NLT) are taken from the Holy Bible, New Living Translation, copyright ©1996, 2004, 2015 by Tyndale House Foundation. Used by permission of Tyndale House Publishers, Carol Stream, Illinois 60188. All rights reserved.

ISBN: 978-1-6642-8147-9 (sc)
ISBN: 978-1-6642-8148-6 (e)

Library of Congress Control Number: 2022919302

Print information available on the last page.

WestBow Press rev. date: 11/15/2022

Thanks to

—Amanda and Hope, who love me enough to give me space to write and create;

—everyone who has demonstrated love to me in so many ways over the years. The compassion, correction, patience, forgiveness, instruction, pride, creativity and empathy that you have demonstrated has built a foundation for me to comprehend the height, depth and width of love that God has for me;

INTRODUCTION

Love seems complicated. Not many people would have the confidence to call themselves a love expert, even though it's probably one topic they have the a lot of experience with. How weird would it be to talk with someone who called him or herself a love expert?

In reality, most of us encounter love from a variety of different people every day of our lives. It's not always perfect, nor do we always recognize it as love, but it's unmistakably there. We receive it from parents, friends, partners, spouses—even my dog communicates love to me when that little tail starts wagging.

Love begins from day one of life, when a parent rearranges everything about his or her life to love and care for a newborn. It means sacrificing sleep, energy, career, hobbies and more, all so this infant gets the love it needs. If you are, or have ever been, a young parent, you know exactly what I'm talking about. You have the bags under your eyes to prove it. The infant might know it's being loved, but everything about what you do for this child is indeed an expression of love.

As we grow into our school-age years, we experience a new kind of love: learning to play and tease other boys and girls on the playground. It's a relational, fun kind of love. We don't have the capacity to understand our childhood interactions as love, but it does indeed teach us about another aspect of it, which is experienced as play. As we mature (and I use that word loosely) into teenagers, boys who used to be yucky and smelly turn into hot topics of conversations in groups of girls, even though for the most part they are still yucky and smelly. With our teenage hormones raging, we learn that love has a passionate side, one that is emotionally driven. It can lead us to do and say things we never imagined we would. But love is indeed emotional. As we grow into young adulthood, we start to pair off, beginning to dream about our futures, and make plans to sacrifice our independence to become one new being with our partner. We make choices about vacation destinations, car types, even clothing choices because true love is not self-serving, it serves the needs and wants of those we love.

Love is deep and complicated and diverse—and, at times, unexplainable. And this describes human love. God's love is indeed all these things but so much more. I did not grow up going to church, so I never really had a good sense of who God was, or what it meant for Him to love me. Our family went to church at Christmas and Easter, but most of my Sundays were focused on sleeping in and playing sports. The best Sundays included brunch at the Best Western with those little breakfast sausages, but either way, Sundays were certainly not to be ruined going to a place where we sat and listened to someone drone on about God. God was for holidays, funerals and people who really needed to change their lives. I was doing OK and didn't need to mess up my weekends with church.

During the time I was in elementary school, my mom became a follower of Jesus, and she went to church a lot more. She would have liked if the whole family had gone with her, but church was just too boring. When we ended up going, I learned the basics: that Jesus and God were apparently the same person, and that Jesus died for me, but it didn't make a whole lot of sense. Clearly, Jesus lived well before I was ever born, so I wasn't too sure how that could be true, and how does dying for someone who didn't need it or ask for it really be all that loving? After all, I seemed like a pretty good kid, so I'm not sure what all the fuss was about, how God had to die because of how bad I was. If God wanted to love me, there were better ways to show it than dying. I needed a new baseball glove, maybe an extended summer, or if he was really feeling generous He could have given us world peace and no more sickness. Now *that* would be a way to show love.

Bible stories of sin, death, judgment and eternity are all overwhelming and didn't make much sense to me as a kid. Actually, they don't make much sense to many adults. If God is so great, why would He send all these perfectly fine human beings, who didn't want to make time for church, straight to hell. I figured if God were that exclusive, I didn't want much to do with Him anyway. I was doing OK on my own.

The stories we've been told about God don't seem very loving, so many of us are not too sure we want to spend much time understanding Him. By the time I reached high school, I had already written off religion. Religious people seemed just as stuck up as God was to me. I was still OK to go to church occasionally, as long as there was food. Or girls. Or sports. Sports, food or girls could get me to participate in church.

But a funny thing started to happen while I was there for those other things. I started to hear, and really process, all those stories about God's love—and more specifically, about how He loved. I started to hear how He *was* love. As it turns out, the Bible was not all about bad people going to hell but how God loved all people and wanted to bring them closer to Him. These stories were really about all the different kinds of love that he demonstrates to us.

Over the next seven years I attended church regularly and even studied theology in college, eventually earning a degree in theology. Who would have guessed that a kid who was bored by church would end up spending every day working in one, and potentially boring other people? Hopefully most of what I share isn't too boring, because since these early days, I've lived my life working for the church, trying to help people understand that the basic idea of

Christianity is not about who can avoid hell but understanding how much God loves us.

Maybe you're like me, and the only parts of God and the church you know are ones that turn you off, such as how people get judged and God gets angry. On behalf of the entire Christian world, we're sorry about that. We have not done the best job over the years of telling the right stories. We've made people think the most important part about God is something other than the love He has for us. "God is love, and all who live in love live in God, and God lives in them" (1 John 4:16).

The story of the Bible is mostly about how much God loves us and describes how God came to earth to be with us and level the playing field between humans and God. His love for us inspired Him to do it for us, so that we in turn could love God, and other people as well. As a church we tend to mess that up, telling too many stories of sin, hell and power, which are indeed discussed in the Bible. But we neglect to share how these are all parts of His great love for us.

I'd love for you to give me the privilege of a few minutes, walking through some of the different ways God loves us. The totality of God's love is so different from anything we've ever experienced in terms of loving each other. Yet in many ways, how we love each other reveals small parts of how He loves us.

Over the pages of this book we'll look at some fun stories and some verses in the Bible that show us how God loves us like

An artist;
A patient grandparent;
A kindergarten teacher;
An in-home caregiver;
An honourable judge;
An empathetic counsellor;
A proud parent;
A broken-hearted love;

A benevolent king;
A jealous spouse; and
An adoptive parent.

To be clear, He is not one of these, he is all of them. To miss His love, in part, means you will not understand the whole. Feel free to jump to any section you'd like to read first, because these concepts don't build off each other. Remember, any chapter you read will be incomplete without the other 10. You can't understand God's judgment as love without understanding his gracious, benevolent style of love. And vice versa, and actually at least eight other concepts as well. So anything you read in this book needs to be taken in concert with everything else you read, or you'll be misled.

Of course, these few pages will not be able to describe the entirety of God's love. There are thousands of books and semester-long courses and hours-long teaching sessions on God's love that still don't do Him justice. But take these stories, and consider the ways God wants to love you, as you see His love revealed in all these people.

CHAPTER 1
A Master Artist Who Includes Himself in the Painting

If you want to understand God and how He loves us, then it's important to go back to the beginning. A great deal of attention is paid these days trying to find ourselves or understand ourselves better by exploring different parts of who we are. We're on a journey to love ourselves because, we're taught, if we don't, it's hard to be loved by another.

So we buy books, complete surveys and go on spiritual retreats, investing countless dollars and energy into self-discovery. We search to know ourselves well so we can love ourselves well. It's an important journey for sure, but if God created us, He should be the one with the best answers to all our questions. If our journey of self-discovery leads us anywhere other than to God, we will end up with a skewed understanding of ourselves. We will end up with a human take on a divine issue. It will be an interpretation of ourselves, without ever knowing if we got it right.

If you've ever been to an art museum, you'll understand this on a greater level. As the crowds look at the pieces on the walls, each gallery participant creates a story about what exactly the artist was trying to convey. We suppose they had deep sadness, which is being expressed through a dull and dark colour palette. Or we can see social commentary being made through placement of characters on the canvas. But without asking the artist, you will only ever really have the tale you've told yourself instead of the truth.

During the Renaissance era, some of the greats began a trend to include their faces in their works of art. In Raphael's *School of Athens*, he is depicting some of the greatest minds of Greek culture: Plato, Pythagoras, Socrates and da Vinci are all depicted in this fictional gathering of the greats. But in the midst of these great intellectuals, we see Raphael. He is in a conversation with the astronomer Zoroaster in the bottom right corner. Zoroaster is holding a globe, and Raphael is beside him, part of this group, in which you would think he would otherwise not belong. Raphael often did this in his works. He made sure the one who created the art was part of the art.

It's kind of an interesting move, to put oneself in the art one is creating. It could be interpreted as a self-serving move, wanting to make sure the world doesn't just see the art but sees the one who created it.

But that was not the intention behind Rafael's or other artists' self-inclusion in their pieces. Using one's own likeness in art allows the art to be humanized. The artists communicated that they see and are working to understand the lives and experiences of their subjects. While Raphael didn't live with Plato or Socrates or almost any of the subjects in his painting, he has a chance to identify with them by imaging himself in their world, what it would have been like to have conversations with them and to share their experiences.

The Bible says we are one of God's greatest works of art. "For we are God's masterpiece. He has created us anew in Christ Jesus, so we can do the good things he planned for us long ago" (Ephesians 2:10 New Living Translation).

This fresco is part of the Vatican's palace. Raphael became a renowned artist by the time he was in his twenties, and he was invited by the pope to live and work in Rome, beautifying the Vatican. This piece alone took two years to complete. If a human artist like Raphael spent that kind of time creating his great works, we can only imagine the kind of painstaking details God invested in making sure He created you the way He wanted.

God spoke to the prophet Jeremiah and told him He knew Jeremiah before he was formed: "I knew you before I formed you in your mother's womb" (Jeremiah 1:5).

Maybe creation took only six days, but the depth of love God has for us means He designs and plans for each of the billions of people alive on this planet. He puts us together in ways that only make sense to Him. And just like Raphael, He puts a piece of Himself in His creation so He can participate in the conversations going on in our world. He invests His image into our lives so He can see and know the conversations going on in our everyday lives and can identify with what we experience. "So God created human beings in his own image" (Genesis 1:27).

You've probably read this before, but have you ever stopped to comprehend it on the level of being part of your journey of self-discovery? When we start to try to understand ourselves, we should, in part, be discovering God and His image in us.

Satan's greatest trick is to take something pure and perfect and create a deceptive illusion of it that looks correct but is just a trick. "He has always hated the truth, because there is no truth in him. When he lies, it is consistent with his character; for he is a liar and the father of lies" (John 8:44 NLT).

There is a sad trend these days. People search to *know* themselves and end up questioning their personality, abilities or even their gender or sexual orientation. We question whether the *mold* God formed us in is right. We get lost going down a path of questioning ourselves rather than understanding God through ourselves.

Let's take that to a deeper level.

In self-discovery, some of us may find that we are lonely and crave a greater human connection. We battle feelings of depression because of isolation or a broken connection. We can question why God would make us feel this way. If we go right back to the creation story, God created men and women because it wasn't good to be alone. God is triune, three persons in one, existing in continual relationship. This path of self-discovery should teach us that like God, a relational connection is deeply critical to satisfaction in life. Our need for relationship teaches us something about how God exists as three in one.

Others may go through self-discovery and learn that life is busy and scattered, and their minds feel overwhelmed. The brokenness of our thoughts robs us of satisfaction in life. And we get angry. But remember the life of Jesus. How many times do we see Jesus escaping from the crowds, or even His friends, so He could have quiet time to think and pray? He demonstrated that to function as God designed, we can't always be in go-mode with people. We'll naturally break down. God hardwired us to require quiet connection time to meet with Him and be restored by His Spirit.

Because of God's attention to detail and desire to include His nature in us, the things that help or hurt us are revelations of God's character to us. The faulty thinking is that anything we discover in ourselves that doesn't feel right is a character flaw that we need to fix. Oftentimes the things that don't feel right are probably more of a reflection of how we've conditioned ourselves to try to let our culture define us, rather than leaning into the plan God has for us as individuals. God made us, on purpose, with love. We shouldn't feel we need to reject anything we discover in ourselves but rather, we should try to understand God's purpose for it.

Even the whole journey or discovering gender and sexuality can reveal something about God. Our world has tried to define male and female in broken ways. In the garden of Eden, before there was sin, there was no hierarchy of men and women. There were no gender roles or freedom inequalities. Together they were tasked with rule and care over everything. Sometime when we do the process of self-discovery, our gender or orientation feels off. We don't fit the construct of what male or female is for our society. That's because our society has created roles for what is male and what is female.

Let's go back to the first few chapters of the Bible to get a better understanding of how God created us. Our culture tries to make men tough and strong—men don't cry, and men should like to work with their hands more than their hearts and feelings. But God didn't create men to like physical work. Physical work and straining was part of the curse of sin that we were given.

"All your life you will struggle to scratch a living from it. It will grow thorns and thistles for you, though you will eat of its grains. By the sweat of your brow will you have food to eat" (Genesis 3:17–19).

It was our brokenness and believing Satan's lie that led God to curse men with physical strife. Similarly, many cultures try to enforce the submissive role of female to male. But this difference is again a result of the sin. "You will desire to control your husband, but he will rule over you" (Genesis 3:16).

God created us as equals, partners who would lead the kingdom He created for us. A true journey of self-discovery must weed through all the junk of sin and human tradition to find the pure creation of God inside us, which understands he loves us. If you're going through a journey of self-discovery, let it bring you back to a creator God that made us *all* in His image, perfectly as He designed. When God made you, trust that He did it on purpose. Because that's the kind of loving creator He is.

God went to great lengths to invest Himself in you. In fact, anyone who is a follower of Jesus is invited to receive His Holy Spirit, which gives us life. "The Spirit of God, who raised Jesus from the dead, lives in you" (Romans 8:11).

Every day you walk around with the life, character and presence of God living in you. As we go on this journey to understand who God is, knowing that He lives in you is probably the first step to having confidence that His love can be understood.

CHAPTER 2
A Patient Grandparent Who Waits for the Child to Mature

Grandparents have this amazing ability to make you feel as if you can do no wrong, while inside your head, you are well aware of all the terribly wrong things you have already done today. They look at you with eyes that say, "Don't worry, I think you're the best!" They listen to your stories, set aside whatever they're doing to make time for you and give hugs that let you know you are loved.

Grandparents are way better than parents! Parents seem to be the opposite. Parents are often too busy to play, tired of all your stories and seem to point out flaws more than they call out your successes!

One of my fondest memories of my grandmother was an afternoon I spent at her house playing with Transformers. My grandma was in her 80s and had lived a very proper life. There were fancy dishes that were to be used whenever there was company, and there was a cover on the chesterfield couch to make sure it stayed pristine. Grandma was always properly dressed, with a matching scarf and broach. Even if the plan was just to watch a baseball game together, Grandma dressed for it.

One afternoon, when we were scheduled to visit, I decided to bring my Transformers to her house. I had figurines of eagles that turned into planes and warriors who doubled as tanks. But the crown jewel of my collection was my Optimus Prime figure, who led all the Transformers. He was by far the coolest thing I owned at the time. Although I doubt this memory is 100 percent accurate (memories tend to work this way, becoming something we colour the way we want them to be), I feel like I remember Grandma getting down on the floor with me, learning about the hierarchy of the transformers, building a hate for the evil Megatron and his band of Decepticons and always respecting the authority, Optimus Prime. She wouldn't dare mess with him. (If none of this makes any sense to you, clearly you were not a young boy in the 1980s.)

And to think that my mom and dad had tried to prevent me from bring toy robots to Grandma's house. They almost seemed annoyed that I would want to play with them with her. Little did they realize how hard-core of a grandma she was!

It's funny how thirty years can pass and a memory like that stands out. Being a parent now I totally realize how frustrating an argument this would have been. "No, Rick, carrying multiple toys with small pieces to your grandmother's house, who has a dog that eats things, is not a good idea. Grandma doesn't care. Bring one to show her, but she's not going to play with you." I can absolutely hear myself saying something similar to my daughter.

I wonder if parents ever get tired of being wrong?

Grandma didn't care that she didn't understand what I was trying to explain to her, she did her best to comprehend what a Transformer was, and then she played with me. She didn't seem to care that all the pieces might not make it back to my house; she was enjoying the moment.

As I continued to grow up, my childhood toys lost their relevance, and the things that occupied the space in my brain were about relationships, schools, jobs and money. Every young adult feels like they, and they alone, know what's best for him. They feel like their parents don't get it and end up getting in their way of trying to be independent. The truth is almost every young adult makes a whole lot of terrible choices that drive their parents up the wall as they see their child going through so much unnecessary pain that they could avoid if they would just receive some advice.

But not their grandparents. Their grandparents don't lose their cool; instead, they take time to listen. They do their best to comprehend what's going on, give a hug and hope it works out. They seem oblivious to the mistakes or the dangers surrounding the choices their grandchildren are making. They're just like they were on the day they got on the floor and played a silly game of Transformers.

The funny thing is that grandparents (by definition) were all parents before they were grandparents. They were once the too busy, too tired, and too mean to want their kids to bring toys with small pieces on family trips. They fought with their young adult kids the same as we do.

So what changed?

Maybe we get soft in our old age.

Or maybe we get wiser. We gain perspective.

We get more like God

I hate to be the bearer of bad news, but your grandparents know you're not perfect. They were once in your shoes and know all about how it is to "fool" old Grandma and Grandpa into thinking that life is perfect and you're never at fault. But remember that grandparents are wise. You don't get dumb as you grow old, you simply choose perspective. A grandparent has the wisdom to say, "I know you make mistakes and I love you anyway."

That's what God's love is like. He sees all our shortcomings but loves us anyway. In the years after Jesus was resurrected, there was regular discussion among his followers and even recorded in the Bible about how His return would be imminent. He had promised His disciples that they would see Him return in the same way they saw Him leave, so they expected Jesus would come back soon.

But as the years passed, like grandparents, the apostles gained perspective. So when people in the Church started to question why

Jesus had not yet returned, Peter was able to offer them the answer in his second letter: "The Lord isn't really being slow about his promise, as some people think. No, he is being patient for your sake. He does not want anyone to be destroyed, but wants everyone to repent" (2 Peter 3:9).

God loves us so much, and He knows there is good in all of us and that we possess the ability to fundamentally change. He delays His return to earth and the beginning of the eternal age so that we have the opportunity to join Him in that perfection. He sees our faults and has the patience to let us mature.

If you can catch a grandparent in a moment of weakness, they'll probably say something like this about his or her grandchild: "My granddaughter really is a great kid. She is enjoying her youth maybe a little too much, but she'll come around. She's a great kid!"

It's the love and trust of a grandparent that understands that kids aren't perfect and often take some time to mature. They see the flaw and wish it wasn't there, but they will allow you to figure it out by success and failure, by learning from others around you and hopefully by eventually asking for help.

It's important that we remember God's patient nature. So many people are afraid to come to church or start to figure out the process of becoming a follower of Jesus because deep down, they know they have made a lot of mistakes. How could a person like us ever be part of a Christian church? It's exactly how these same flawed individuals can come to Grandma's house when it's time for Christmas dinner. Grandma knows. Grandma cares. But Grandma chooses to love and include anyway.

God knows what you've done. He cares about it deeply. But He chooses to offer forgiveness at any moment and wants to see you join His family at the table.

Too many Christians try to be parents who correct and give consequences to their children when they see them doing wrong. And while it's true that God is described as our Father (we'll get to that part of His love in later chapters), there are still large pieces of God's love that is much more like a grandparent. We've done our world a disservice by actively trying to point out everyone's shortcomings and the mistakes they make. It has made the church, and consequently people's perception of God, to be that of a punitive or angry dad.

But many days God is more like your grandfather. He gets it, but He chooses love anyway. He knows you'll come around one day. "But you, O Lord, are a God of compassion and mercy, slow to get angry and filled with unfailing love and faithfulness (Psalm 86:15).

CHAPTER 3
A Kindergarten Teacher Who Gives You Simple and Basic Ways to Encounter Things of Great Depth

Have you ever tried to read the entire Bible? Some people try to do it each year. Others will set aside two to three months to take it all in. For some it seems like the challenge of a lifetime. But however long it takes you to read the Bible, one thing that is common for all of us: there seem to be so many rules. The first few books of the Bible are packed full of laws for eating, worship, day-to-day life, religious festivals, marriage and family.

In total, there are 613 laws that the Jewish priests, teachers and devout religious people tried to keep. The name given to the collection of these laws is the Mitzvot. These laws became nearly impossible for the Jewish leaders to keep, much less the entire nation. Honouring God feels very heavy when you read this part of the Bible.

But if you really want to take it up a level, try reading the New Testament and properly understanding that God's laws extend to not only your actions, but your thoughts have the ability to break His law. You can cross a boundary in your mind, which makes you just as guilty in God's eyes as if you had crossing the physical boundary. Paul talks about how people who gossip or have bad thoughts are not worthy of entering the kingdom of heaven.

How on earth are any of us supposed to keep all these laws if even our thoughts are being policed? If we can't live up to God's standards, then why on earth would God love people like us?

God's love for us is like a preschool teacher. He understands that we don't fully comprehend how to make Him happy or keep all these rules straight in our minds. So when Moses was up on the mountain in the wilderness, God narrowed it down to ten easier-to-understand phrases for how to honour God, and He wrote them into two stone tablets making up the ten commandments. These 10 are larger categories for the grouping of the 613 laws. If you uphold the one commandment on the tablet, you uphold the group. The groupings of laws contain more than 100 sublaws found in the 613 Mitzvot of Mosaic law.

So at least you can rest assured that you don't need to figure out all 613; just focus on the 10.

But even the ten commandments are based on five principles that were given on two tablets. The first tablet is about how we relate to God, our creator, or our parents. You can call these our vertical relationships.

1. You must not have any other gods but me;
2. You will not make idols;
3. You will not misuse the name of the Lord;
4. You will remember the Sabbath and keep it holy;
5. You will honour your father and mother;

The next five are how we relate to other people in the world. Let's call them our peers or horizontal relationships:

6. You must not murder;
7. You must not commit adultery;

8. You must not steal;
9. You must not lie; and
10. You must not covet.

The laws were given to Moses when he was on the mountain, and they were to help provide the rules of life of how Israel was to set up their new country (when they eventually got there four decades later).

But why did God give Moses two tablets? Wouldn't it make more sense to use a smaller tablet font and give it to him on one tablet? He was carrying it up and down the mountain, for goodness sake, and the Jews would have to cart if across the wilderness for 40 years. Why two tablets?

If you juxtapose the first and second tablets, you see one principle.

Commandments one and six, two and seven, three and eight, four and nine and five and ten all have similar guiding principles.

Commandments one and six are about honouring God and His image in humanity.

Commandments two and seven are about honouring sacred relationships.

Commandments three and eight are about stealing possessions or glory from God.

Commandments four and nine relate to truth, bearing truth to God on the sabbath and speaking truthfully.

Commandments five and ten are about control, and trusting God or our caregivers to know what's best and to provide for us.

Jewish children over the centuries learned this symmetry as they grew, but it is often lost on us in Western churches. But God established principles of how we would live when it comes to our relationship to Him and our relationship to others.

It started with 613. Was grouped in ten. But really was based on five principles.

In the end, when Jesus walked the earth and taught and made disciples, He boiled it all down to two larger groups.

1. Love God;
2. Love others.

> "You must love the Lord your God with all your heart, all your soul, and all your mind." This is the first and greatest commandment. A second is equally important: "Love your neighbor as yourself." The entire law and all the demands of the prophets are based on these two commandments. (Matthew 22:37–40)

God loves you so much that He wanted to make it easy for you to please Him. He took 613 laws, grouped them into 10 sections, separated those 10 sections based on 5 principles and then summed them up in two easy statements to simplify the process of how to honour God.

If you want to love God well, do two things: Love God and love people. You can spend a lifetime breaking down the principles of the other 613 laws and ten commandments, but if you start with these two, you'll be well on your way to honouring God. Jesus was teaching us that the principles behind every law we read in the Bible stem from two things: Love god, and love others.

God's love is like a preschool teacher who knows that maybe one day you will be a scientist or an engineer, and you'll need to understand the deeper principles of algebra, exponents and calculus. As you progress through school, you'll start to zero in on how deep you need to go on some subjects, and how other subjects you need to understand at a high level. So if one day you get there and discover that it might be helpful for you, that's fantastic. Keep going! Most of us will never understand it all.

But for now, the teacher understands that all you need to know is that when you put one and one together, you get two.

And if you put two and two together, you get four.

And if you put two and two and two together—wait for it—you get six!

Start there, fully get it and the rest can be discovered later if/when you need it.

Even though religious scholars can identify 613 ways to honour God well, Jesus wanted to simplify it for us as we get started. If you can get the two concepts, that to please God and serve Him well really only requires loving Him with everything you've got, and loving other people the same way, then you'll be well on your way to pleasing God with your life.

CHAPTER 4

An in-Home Caregiver Who Comes to You Rather Than Makes You Come to Him

A hospital can be a terrifying place. Not even considering that the reason you are there is because you are hurt or sick, the building itself can be intimidating.

The hospital in my neighbourhood has multiple floors, and the floor I walk into from the street level is not floor one. Right off the bat I am already confused and a little lost as to where I go for help. How come floor one isn't floor one? They lay it out in all different wings, like a maze (or a prison). They label those wings A-H, and they do not appear to go in any kind of alphabetical order. Arrows on the floor lead me to all kinds of places I don't want to go, but at times I find myself following those arrows, believing they can lead the way for me, because at least I'll end up at a registration desk that can point me to a new set of arrows to follow. Even getting to and from the hospital is a bit of a mess. I never know if north entrance B is better than west entrance C, and it's more expensive to park there than downtown on a Saturday night. And when I'm ready to leave, I feel like by the time locate the proper exit, and then I find my car in the parking garage, I've spent another $10 walking around trying to get out of the place.

Everyone at the hospital seems rushed, busy and stressed, and for a place that is supposed to be the centre of help to receive care and support, it seems to do the opposite. Obviously, some wonderful people work in hospitals, and I know they are indeed trying their best to serve our communities. But it seems like there is too much need and too few caregivers, and the hospital is stressing out those who work there and those coming to visit.

There must be a better way to do this.

In the past decade or so, there has been a resurgence in home-based care workers who come and deliver the care people need in the quiet and comfort of their home. While doctors aren't arriving to do major surgeries, we're seeing a shift in the healthcare industry, to make space for doctors, nurses and other healthcare professionals to attend to their patients at home to deliver all kinds of services. Blood tests, pain management, occupational therapy, social work, home births and even something like an X-ray can now be available in a home-based service.

While obviously this is much less convenient for the caregiver, the fact that the patient doesn't have to navigate the frustration of the hospital can be the difference between them receiving care or not. When faced with the decision between having to regularly navigate the circus of the local hospital, or simply live through the pain, many individuals choose the latter.

This reality caused many healthcare professionals to ask, "Can we reorganize our system, at our own expense and inconvenience, so that we can provide care to the people who are experiencing challenges to receive it?"

If the focus of the healthcare system was to make it easier for themselves, then they should build larger and more centralized hospitals. But if the focus is removing barriers so that everyone who needs care can receive it, bringing the care to the patients had to be considered. Sometimes home care can even be viewed as an initial step, to build trust with clients who might need to eventually come to the hospital for greater levels of care. But taking the first step to come into clients' homes and space removes the barrier that exists to good care.

The entire story of Jesus, God incarnate, coming to earth to demonstrate His love for us is exactly this type of love. God's perfection made it so that we were unable to be close to Him. Anyone with sin could not enter the presence of a Holy God. It was our barrier to receiving His love. God instituted the system of animal sacrifices being offered by priests to consecrate themselves. Even then, it was allowed once a year, and only by the high priest of the nation. "But only the high priest ever entered the Most Holy Place, and only once a year. And he always offered blood for his own sins and for the sins the people had committed in ignorance" (Hebrews 9:7 NLT).

While this allowed God's people to have a semblance of His care, God knew that more must be done to truly allow people to know His love. So Jesus came to earth, 100 percent God, and 100 percent human at the same time. God sacrificed, and inconvenienced Himself to show us His love.

Just days before Jesus's eventual ascension and return to heaven, there is a beautiful exchange between Peter and Jesus. If you're familiar with the Bible, you will know that right before Jesus's arrest, Peter promised Jesus that he was willing to die to protect Jesus if anyone attacked Him. Even if every other disciple turned away, Peter would remain faithful. Of course it was mere hours later that Peter swore up and down to the angry crowds of Jewish leaders who had arrested Jesus that he was not only *not* a disciple of Jesus, he didn't even know who Jesus was. Jesus and Peter locked eyes in this moment of denial, reminding Peter of how far short he was of the promises he had made earlier in the evening.

Jesus would be crucified that morning, and the two would not speak again. That is, until after Jesus's resurrection, where there is a moment the two meet. The larger group of 11 disciples had breakfast on the beach, and Jesus stole Peter away from the other 10 and asked: "Simon son of John, do you love me more than these?" (John 21:15 NLT). This is a fascinating question for so many reasons. For more than a year now, Jesus had been using the new name he had given Simon: Peter. Peter means *rock*, and Jesus told him it would be on this rock that he would build His church. But on this day, he goes back to his name Simon. And the word Jesus uses for love is the Greek *agape*, which means unconditional love. He says, "… Simon Peter, "Simon son of John, do you *love* me more than these?[a]"

"Yes, Lord," Peter replied, "you know I love you…" (John 21:15)

But the word for love Peter responds with is a different kind of love. He is using the Greek word for love, *philos*, or *phileo*. Jesus asks, "Do you love me unconditionally," and Peter responds, "I love you like a brother."

Jesus asks him a second time, but in this instance he removed Simon's new name, and addresses him by his former name.

"Jesus repeated the question: "Simon son of John, do you love me?" "Yes, Lord," Peter said, "you know I love you." (John 21:16).

Jesus is still using the Greek word agape, but poor Simon Peter can only ashamedly respond by basically saying, "Yes, I love you, but it's not unconditional. It's the love of a brother. Jesus, you know very well that I can't say my love come without condition, because I demonstrated that there are times I won't act in love."

So when Jesus asks the third time, he changes how he asks Peter. In verse 17, we read: "A third time he asked him, 'Simon, son of John, do you love me?'" (John 21:17).

But the word He uses this time is not agape. It's phileo. Jesus comes down to the level of Peter and asks him the question that he knows Peter can answer. He says, "Peter, do you love me like a brother?"

Eventually, Peter's love for Jesus grew into agape-style love. He shared the love of God boldly with the entire world, and it would eventually cost Peter his life, once and for all proving that Peter had unconditional agape-style love. But for it to grow to that space, Jesus had to come to Peter's level. Jesus came to earth to make it easier for us to receive His love. The barriers were too much, and many who needed to know that they were loved simply couldn't access it.

The whole reason Jesus came to earth was to make a way for his created sons and daughters to know Him and receive His love and care. "God showed how much he loved us by sending his one and only Son into the world so that we might have eternal life through him" (1 John 4:9).

Right now there might still be barriers to you understanding how much God loves you. It's important that we see the perspective of God's love, that He not only inconvenienced Himself by coming to earth, He asks us to make a commitment of love that we are presently capable of making. He knows there is probably a greater commitment we can make down the road, and that to receive the full scope of His care, we'll need to follow Him (maybe even navigate the mess that is the hospital parking lot!). But in this moment, like He did with Peter, He asks you whether you can commit to receiving the love at the level you presently understand it.

CHAPTER 5
An Honourable Judge Who Draws Clear Boundaries That Are Not Supposed to Be Challenged

A judge is an intimidating person. She has the power to grant freedom or sentence captivity. Her ruling might cost you thousands of dollars or remand you to counselling or education courses. You present your story to a judge in a way that convinces him or her of your innocence, or at least makes the judge see you in a favourable light. I can remember each time I have sat in front of judges in my life: explaining why I was driving too fast, or discussing implications for my family because of the upcoming ruling. Even when I've been assured that things will go my way, my palms sweat, my heart pounds and I imagine all the terrible things that could happen if the ruling goes against me.

Judges are tasked with upholding order in our society and making decisions that will be forever viewed as fair, regardless of whether we believe it to be fair. Other people will form opinions about you and me based on what the judge determines to be right and fair.

That's a lot of responsibility for one person to handle. And there are a lot of people in the world who want no part of having a judge in their lives.

But God's love is indeed like a judge. The Bible is the story of God and how He loves us, from creation, to incarnation, to death and resurrection, to the gift of the Holy Spirit and finally to the promise of His return. It details how He loves us but also His expectations for us.

When Jesus was teaching about right and wrong to the church leaders, He said, "But I say, love your enemies! Pray for those who persecute you! [...] But you are to be perfect, even as your Father in heaven is perfect" (Matthew 5:44, 48).

He further explained: "Unless your righteousness is better than the righteousness of the teachers of religious law and the Pharisees, you will never enter the kingdom of heaven!" (Matthew 5:20).

In this way, God our judge has seen our lives, been able to determine that we are less than perfect and rendered a verdict that we our guilty. And we're guilty in so many ways. It's not just about what we do, it's also about what we neglect to do, or even how we think sometimes.

> You have heard that our ancestors were told, "You must not murder. If you commit murder, you are subject to judgment." But I say, if you are even angry with someone, you are subject to judgment! If you call someone an idiot, you are in danger of being brought before the court. And if you curse someone, you are in danger of the fires of hell. (Matthew 5:21–22)

In fact, if you read the Bible back to front, there are rules for what we eat and when we work versus when we rest; how we handle our money; our sexual lives and orientation; our language and our worship; how we make promises and how we conduct business. Regardless of whether we agree with the rules He set, we are judged by these rules. Although He gives us the kindergarten level of understanding all the laws into 10, the 613 laws exist for a reason. The longer we follow God, the greater insight we should strive to gain so we can more intimately know God, our Creator.

When a person is first introduced to God, the judgment aspect of His love is often enough to make many people want little to do with God or Christianity. It seems so many rules are designed to limit us. And with a standard of perfection required to please God, what's the point of even trying to follow them if we'll be guilty with even one wrong thought?

If we take a step back, we can learn that God's rules communicate love for us. If you dig under the surface of the rule, you'll discover that the rules He judges us by are designed to give us the most fulfilling life we could imagine.

Look at the law of the Sabbath, for instance. In the 10 commandments, we are instructed to do no work on that day. God worked for six days, and even God rested for a day. So obviously His creation needs rest as well. In this overscheduled and overconnected world, we can all understand the need for rest. The Jewish leaders developed rules to restrict cooking, harvesting, doing business and even cleaning. Some devout religious people would try to do absolutely nothing, barely moving on the Sabbath. Now that seems a little farfetched.

But consider it for a moment. What if, on one day every week, no one expected you to check in on work emails. No one needed you to run out to the store, because all the stores were closed. Church was not a thing to "get finished," because it was literally the only thing on your calendar for that day. One day. Every week. Just worship and then rest. And it's not a rule to try to keep, it's a gift given to you to have balance. Breaking it is indeed counting against you, but embracing it is restorative to you.

The rules around sex and marriage and sexual orientation are often viewed as a big barrier for people to embrace God as well. Our world has embraced a worldview that encourages people to lean into every sexual feeling or thought they have and explore it. The theory is that in this exploration, you will discover your true self, and in the end, find true happiness.

But so many of us look deep within and see some broken thought processes and feelings. If we followed every one of them, we'd end up living a life with multiple sexual partners, in multiple levels of commitment.

God had a different plan for our protection. That two people would make a lifelong commitment to each other. They would develop a life where they could confidently trust each other without ever fearing being left or cheated on. Through the ups and downs, the partners would defer to each other, choosing love for each other first rather than choosing to care for their own needs. The boundary of marriage is to give us happiness and fulfillment, not to restrict us.

It's human nature to focus on a boundary. The boundary, or the rule, always feels restrictive. We question why we need boundaries. And we push against them. But if we could get ourselves into the headspace that we trusted that God has purpose for these boundaries, we'd open ourselves up to experience a new aspect of His love. His rules.

Because there is one more rule that God works into our lives. Anyone who is brave enough to admit he or she has not lived up to the standard of perfection and believes that through Jesus, God grants forgiveness for shortcomings, is granted immunity from any penalty. "For the wages of sin is death, but the free gift of God is eternal life through Christ Jesus our Lord" (Romans 6:23).

Our shortcomings never really have to be counted against us if we follow this one simple rule: To accept the gift offered to us by our Judge. Because God is not a vindictive Judge, pointing out all the places we've gone wrong. He is an honourable and righteous Judge who wants to make a ruling in our favour. In fact, when He saw things were going so wrong, He came to earth to change things up.

When we look at all the rules listed out for us in the Bible, we need to view them with the lens of love. They are not boundaries put there to restrict us or to lead us to a place of blame or shame. They are guidelines to help us get the maximum out of this life. And when we cross them, it's OK. God has made a made a way for us to be restored back into His expectation of perfection.

CHAPTER 6

An Empathetic Counsellor Who Invites You to Come Away from the Heaviness of Your Life and Unpack Some of What You Are Tired of Carrying Around

For years it was always thought that the strongest among us never needed support. We idolized the individuals who appeared self-made and never needed extra support to accomplish things. Thankfully, we have moved forward as a society and arrived at the place where, at the very least, it's OK to say you need help, before getting into situations where we are over our heads. The counselling profession has exploded, and we have psychotherapists, coaches, counsellors, psychiatrists and all kinds of specialized therapists who work with clients to help them achieve the success they dream of. With the explosion taking place in the industry, many counsellors find themselves overbooked but still taking on new clients every week out of need. Our society has embraced the necessity for good counsel.

If you're new to the world of counselling, you might think a good counsellor gives you the answers you need, and then you solve your challenges based on this good advice. But that would require every counsellor to be an expert in every area of challenge that anyone could ever face. It would mean all counsellors are super humans with answers that seem to be hiding away from the public, unable to access these solutions for themselves. A number of years ago I went back to school and studied for Masters in psychology and have counselled for over ten years now and I can attest that we are not super humans, nor experts at life.

Counsellors are experts in how humans think and how the brain works. Through training, we can more easily identify patterns of thought or behaviour that might be causing challenges to an individual's life. While they may not have a specific solution for each individual problem faced, a skilled counsellor can help identify the issue that is leading to problem. Then the role of a counsellor is to help an individual create a unique solution that will be helpful. While it may not be helpful for the next person, it is helpful for that person because he or she created it! Counselors are psychology experts. But you are an expert in you.

I've spent many sessions with people, empathizing, reflecting and laying out the issue, only to end up in a space where we look at each other, thinking, *Well, what are we going to do?* They expect me to have the answer, but I'm looking right back them, ready to help them create their own answer. Clearly, I recognize that they're not ready to solve their issue on their own, or why would they be meeting with me in the first place? But deep down, I know their challenge will only get solved when they are intricately involved in creating the solution.

Change only happens when a person feels motivated to change and comfortable with the process. What's motivational and comfortable for me will be different from what's motivational and comfortable for you. We spend time together, looking at what steps they feel comfortable taking as first steps, defining end goals and the process starts to become clear and manageable.

God's love is a lot like a counsellor. He makes Himself available to you, whenever you need it, even if it's just to come and be heard. He is not going to give you solutions right away about everything in your life that you need to change. He is ready to sit with you, in some of the hard spaces, and help you reflect.

One of my favourite passages in the Bible that describes the heart and mission of Jesus is found in Matthew: "Come to me, all you who are weary and burdened, and I will give you rest. Take my yoke upon you and learn from me, for I am gentle and humble in heart, and you will find rest for your souls. For my yoke is easy and my burden is light" (Matthew 11:28–30).

It begins with a call for people who are having a hard time in life, anyone who is weary or burdened or tired and carrying something heavy. These days we carry so much that is beyond our capacity. We carry the hurt of generations past, who mistreated others and left our world inequitable. We carry the weight of managing the future so the next generation will have a world in which to exist. We have jobs that ask for more time than we have, and bills that amount to more money than we dream of making. We have relationships that have become more complicated, and identity issues that seem unsolvable. Yes, I think we all could be described at one point or another as weary and burdened. And Jesus the counselor invites us to come to Him.

When we come to Him, He promises rest. This sentence can also be translated as "and I will rest you." It's an active verb that Jesus uses, meaning He will do the work of making sure we are rested.

Rest is a common theme throughout the Bible, with one of the main references to rest being heaven. Psalm 95:11 declares it, and Hebrews 4:4 echoes it: that to be in God's presence in heaven is our rest. But here, Jesus uses that same word, inviting us to come to Him and He will give us an experience of this rest: a piece of heaven on earth.

And then Jesus contrasts the idea of work and rest. He says that we are to take his yoke on. The common understanding is that a yoke is the piece of plough that attaches the oxen to one another and to the cart, working the field. But a Hebrew understanding of this word is different: a yoke was the total of a rabbi's teaching. A student would be yoked to the rabbi's work and teaching. This interpretation makes more sense in this teaching, as Jesus says we are to come and learn from Him.

This is the part of the verses where Jesus demonstrates His work as a counselor. Normally, when we seek counsel from a wise teacher, we expect to be wowed, or blown away a little. After all, a teacher has wisdom, and a great teacher like Jesus should have wisdom that would oppose some of the things we've always thought to be true.

Having your perspective on truth can be difficult, even unsettling for some. But Jesus says that His teaching is gentle and humble. While it may oppose what we've known to be true, He is not oppositional. In the truth of Jesus we are able to find rest for our souls when we are tired. And it's the kind of rest that is only found in heaven. The kind of rest you get when there is no pain, no stress, no sadness and no failure. Jesus gently and humbly invites you to enter this rest.

Many of us work hard all our lives to create an existence that provides us with the ability to rest. We work hard and save so we can take holidays. We try to buy a home that creates a space to unwind. We want a job that gives us proper work-life balance. It's so much work to try to find rest. And then, in the middle of it, we hear the voice of Jesus, inviting us to come and enter His rest at no cost at all. The pathway to rest is different than the way everyone else seems to be going, and Jesus will never forcefully make you go His way.

But He does offer this invitation: "Let me guide you in the way of peace and rest, regardless of the life you have created for yourself. You've been working so hard, and it all seems so heavy. But my yoke, my way is easy and light."

He loves us enough not to be forceful. But like a good counselor, Ge is ready to guide us. When you feel like life has defeated you, or you have failed, the last thing you need is one more person pointing out where things went wrong. You turn to a counsellor who offers a safe place, a listening ear and an opportunity to reflect. We have such a gracious, heavenly Father who knows we will find ourselves down and defeated at times, and He offers us the safe and easy space to come and just be with Him. Today might not be the day you need God to fix all the world's problems for you; you need Him to remind you that He is with you in the midst of them.

CHAPTER 7

A Proud Parent Who Chooses to Not Focus on the Flaws in His or Her Child but Only Sees the Good

I've worked with many groups of children over the years. I've been a camp counsellor, a youth worker, a school volunteer and a church program leader. Anyone who spends any amount of time with large groups of kids will see some of the most unbelievable things take place.

I once volunteered in a primary school classroom, and the kids participated in a bucket drum circle for their music class. I have celebrated the change in primary school away from the recorder to bucket drumming. Every sibling in my family had to learn to play the recorder, which is possibly the most annoying wind instrument on the face of the earth. It's almost impossible to play anything on the recorder that anyone will enjoy. The music it makes is loud and screechy, and every fourth note comes out like a high-pitched squeal because the bottom hole covered by your thumb is always poorly constructed. God bless my parents for what was nine years of recorder practice in their home. Nobody deserves to hear "Three Blind Mice" played on a recorder for nine straight years. That's just wrong.

Anyway, these kids were participating in the new primary school music trend, the drum circle. Everyone gets a giant blue pail and a pair of heavy drumsticks, and you bang on the sides, bottom and rim to make a variety of sounds, attempting to keep some kind of rhythm. I'm not saying it's Beethoven, but it's better than the recorder.

On this day, one of the lovely little girls must have looked at this other little girl the wrong way, or shot her a glare of sorts because her classmate picked up her bucket and smacked the first girl across the face, sending her flying to the ground! At this point, chaos erupted and others felt the need to come to their friends' defense. One particularly justice-oriented young lady grabbed her compass, opened up the sharp end and stabbed the arm of the bucket whacker! And these are grade 1 girls.

Angels.

Long story short, the fight was broken up quite quickly, and aside from a small hole in the forearm and a sore cheek, everyone was able to walk away from the scene under her own power. Of course trying to describe the series of events later to the parents was another mess altogether.

The parent tried to help us understand that we must have been mistaken. There was no way "her" little girl was capable of picking up a bucket and swinging it at another girl like a club. And while the other parent admitted that it's possible that her daughter could maybe, potentially, have stabbed this other child, she probably meant well as she was coming to the defense of the first girl.

I know what I saw. I saw these little angels turn into monsters and attacked each other like trained fighters. How could the parents, who spend hours with their children every day, never have seen any of this kind of behaviour before? Over the course of my years with kids I've heard insults hurled at me because I had whole-wheat goldfish crackers for snack rather than the *real* goldfishes. I've seen temper tantrums erupt over who messed up the paly dough, and once I watched a young man pee his pants intentionally because he was not allowed to leave the room to go to the washroom at a given notice.

Kids are great—really, they are. But I know that even the best-behaved children can act out in outrageous ways, so I go back to my original question: How can these parents find it so unbelievable that their child lost their mind for minute and got a little stabby/whacky?

But when the average parent attempts to describe the characteristics of his or her own child, words like hardworking, resilient, obedient and compliant come up. I gave up working with kids because I'd yet to discover one child who matched the parent's description.

Parents aren't blind to all this, they just have a different lens. They experience the bad just as much as kids' workers and teachers do, but it's not what sticks out in their memory. It's the good stuff that stays with them. Sure no child is perfect, but when you look deep inside, beyond some of the exterior, you can see beautiful human beings inside anyone (even bucket whackers!).

God's love for us is like that. We all have rather high opinions of ourselves. Me particularly—I like to think I'm kind and generous. I've donated to people on the street and held the door at the mall more than my share of the time. I've been polite when I am frustrated with a telemarketer, and I've even paid for someone else at Tim Horton's when they couldn't find their wallet. I'm an awesome human!

I've also lost my temper and yelled at someone who cut me off on the road. I've altered the truth when the truth didn't make me sound like a great guy. In my teenage years I stole from the store and swore at others.

I may not have hit anyone else in the face with a bucket, but when I was a goalie in hockey I knocked out a few teeth with my blocker because somebody came in my crease.

Maybe I'm not such an awesome human after all.

Yet God looked at me and my life, and even before I asked forgiveness for all the bad ways I act and thoughts I think, He made a plan to smooth it all over. "But God showed His great love for us by sending Christ to die for us while we were still sinners" (Romans 5:8).

He sees the stuff that is unlovable in me and chooses to love me anyway. Religion is all about trying to make ourselves acceptable to God. We feel like maybe if we can act good enough to impress God, He will be fooled into thinking we're altogether good and not see the other stuff. But it's when we embrace the fact that we're not perfect and that there is a lot about us that is "unlovely," and recognize that God loves us perfectly in spite of these things that we actually understand God as our Father. It's because God has a lens of love for each of us that no other person has. God sees our lives through the lens of the forgiveness of Jesus, allowing Him to love what seems otherwise unlovable.

I've always thought that these parents are totally blind to what is reality. Maybe they've got the Father's heart in them. Loving what is lovable in their kids, despite the unlovely pieces that others can see in them

Paul is the Bible hero who figured this out in a profound way. He was a person who persecuted believers of Jesus, even to the point of killing them because they were messing up his religion. But after a powerful encounter with God, Paul began to realize what the Father's love is like. "This is a trustworthy saying, and everyone should accept it: 'Christ Jesus came into the world to save sinners'—'and I am the worst of them all'" (1 Timothy 1:15).

One of Jesus's last lessons on earth was His demonstration of love to Peter. He told his closest friends that he was going to be arrested and eventually killed. Peter, a passionate and zealous follower, corrected Jesus, saying this should never and could never happen. Jesus sadly had to look at Peter and say: "I tell you the truth, Peter—this very night, before the rooster crows, you will deny three times that you even know me" (Matthew 26:34).

Of course these events took place hours before Peter watched Jesus get arrested. He was fearful of his own arrest and swore up and down in front of the crowd that he did not know who Jesus was, let alone a follower of his teaching. How disheartening this must have been for the human heart of Jesus. The man in whom Jesus had invested three years of his life, teaching him the deeper things of the kingdom and the ways of God, was not even willing to be identified as one who had been around Jesus.

And when the rooster crowed following Peter's third denial, he and Jesus locked eyes, and Peter ran away, recognizing that there was something unlovable about him.

Yet Jesus still loved Peter enough to die for him. To come back to him after His resurrection and teach him about loving others. There is a famous interaction between Jesus and Peter on the beach some days after Jesus resurrection. Three times Jesus asks Peter if he truly loves him. Each time Peter responds by saying yes, of course I do. Some have compared the three denials, meaning that Peter needed to prove his love for Jesus equally three times. But that's not the way of Jesus. Jesus loves the lovable parts of us, and has looked past the faults.

No, I see Jesus's questions as more of a teaching moment. He seemed to be saying, Peter, if you love me, then you must go and demonstrate this same kind of love to my other children. Love them with the same love that I have loved you with. Feed their souls with only things that will ensure they will never hunger again. Feed them with this kind of deep love that only sees the beauty, not the faults.

I'm not saying bucket-whacking is a good idea.

I am saying the bucket-whacker is lovable.

That's God's love for you.

CHAPTER 8
A Broken-Hearted Love Who Needs to Hear I'm Sorry Every so Often

I met my future wife when I was twelve years old. My best friend's family were good friends with her family so we crossed paths every few months when I was at my friend's house and her family came by. I knew her name and had endured a few conversations with her over the years, but girls were annoying to me until I was twelve. She really was just an obstacle in the way of my friend and me enjoying an afternoon of sports together. His parents made us include her, so that meant we had to do something less fun.

But by age thirteen, something changed. Suddenly, spending time with girls seemed a lot less lame, and I was happy to include her in what the plans were for the day. And as we started to spend time together, it turned out I kinda liked her.

Over the next couple of years we hung out here and there and eventually decided to make it official (or at least as official as fifteen-year-olds who live in different cities before the Internet existed can make things).

We met at thirteen, got together by fifteen and married by twenty-three. Never looked back once!

Well … maybe once.

There was a period of a few months where we kinda weren't together (mutual decision), and I tried to see if there were any other girls worth liking (not so mutual a decision). Turns out there was another girl out there who wasn't half bad, so I spent a little time with her. Eventually I came to my senses, and Amanda and I found our way back together. We haven't looked back since. Not even twice!

No one can or should expect a teenaged romance to work perfectly, and thankfully she only reminds me of my failure every three to four weeks when she needs leverage over me. But what I learned over those few months making my way back to Amanda was that she was going to need to hear the words "I'm sorry." I had all kinds of good reasons for what had happened.

We weren't together.

We had agreed mutually to move on.

I was only fifteen, and my brain was still developing.

But even though all those things were true, I'm sorry still needed to be said. And as it turns out, there have been many more times in the course of our three decades together when "I'm sorry" needed to be said. Big things and little things.

Even in hard times, it's not as if our love for each other changes. But the act of acknowledging a mistake, as well as acknowledging the choice the other is making to offer forgiveness so freely is an important piece in a love-filled relationship. *She doesn't have to forgive me; she wants to forgive me!* There's a big difference there. It's not like my pleas of forgiveness enact some big sequence that end with a begrudging, "Fine, I'll forgive you. This time." The humble acknowledgment of wrong opens the door to the grace-filled forgiveness to be a piece that connects us in an even greater way.

God's love for us is a lot like a spouse who is ready and willing to forgive the moment we're ready to engage in this part of His love. I think we've misunderstood part of God's forgiveness process over the years. We've viewed it in a punitive light. God becomes this dictator-type personality who will pardon us if we can subject ourselves to the demeaning experience of admission of sin. "But if we confess our sins to him, he is faithful and just to forgive us our sins and to cleanse us from all wickedness" (1 John 1:19).

This can sound like a contractual exchange, with all the power being managed by God. But reimagine forgiveness as already being expected in the relationship and is part of the understanding of love. God isn't looking to forgive people who earn it. His entire purpose of coming to earth was to have everyone experience this kind of forgiveness. "For this is how God loved the world: He gave His one and only Son, so that everyone who believes in Him will not perish but have eternal life. God sent His Son into the world not to judge the world, but to save the world through Him" (John 3:16–17).

Jesus's purpose on earth was not judgment but salvation. He came because He knows we knew we didn't measure up, and we're sorry about that. His sacrifice on the cross was His expression of the acceptance of our guilt, for the purpose of forgiveness. Of course for it to be a healthy relationship, we still need to participate in the act of asking for it, but He's ready to offer it to any of us.

Shame is a terrible emotion that humans struggle with, especially when someone heaps it on us. When we feel like less than enough, or that we somehow don't measure up, a deep hurt or sadness stays with us. I've had many counselling clients over the year who are truly broken by the experience of shame, and it takes years of work to rebuild one's self-esteem and self-perception as being worthy or even *just enough*.

The mistake Christianity has made over the years is communicating God's need for holiness from us, with a feeling of shame for our sin. Basically, if we feel bad about what we've done, then God will love us. That's a textbook example of how to send someone into a shame cycle. "So now there is no condemnation for those who belong to Christ Jesus" (Romans 8:1).

It can't be overstated enough that a forgiving relationship with Jesus is not focused on our guilt. Long before we recognize our guilt, He's already prepared to forgive us. The beautiful part of this relationship is found in entering forgiveness by asking for it. It may seem subtle, but when it releases you from the idea of shame, it's truly significant. Regularly admitting a shortcoming has the power to build greater trust and intimacy than it does to bring shame and guilt. Whether we refer to our relationship with our spouse or heavenly Father, if we keep the relationship safe enough to be able to admit our shortcomings, we will inevitably grow closer as the years go by.

I know there is no way Amanda would have married me if her standard was that I could never make a mistake or let her down. That ship sailed when we were teens. Don't tell her, but she's not always perfect either (shhh). Marriage only works when it's based on the principle of forgiveness being continually offered.

We the church are called the bride of Christ. Paul writing in the New Testament described our relationship as a marriage relationship as well. I guess it's because there are so many lessons from marriage that copy over to our connection with God. He loves you. Unconditionally. Just don't forget to talk about how He loves you every so often by saying you're sorry.

Trust me—you'll like what you hear back.

CHAPTER 9
A Benevolent King Who Welcomes People Who Don't Seem to Deserve His Love

Experiencing my religious growing up in Canada means I have a Westernized understanding of Jesus and the Bible. Much of the nuance of what Jesus taught is totally lost on a person like me. The essence of the truth is still plain, but the subtleties get lost. It's kind of like the experience of listening to a jazz musician. I've heard it said that the best jazz players often leave out the notes that they want you to hear, so it's the notes that they are not playing that make it so great. I tend to listen to music for the notes I hear, so jazz seems lost on me. I can appreciate the rhythm and the creativity to whatever is being played, but the refined ear can differentiate between what is good or great and what is truly a unique piece of music.

One of the best parables to comprehend God's grace and compassionate love is found in Luke 15. It's preceded by two parables about things that were lost and then celebrated when they were found: a lost coin and a lost sheep. (Luke 15: 1-10) These three make up what's called the Lost Parables Trilogy.

The first two are straightforward. They tell of a shepherd and a

GOD'S LOVE IS LIKE...

homeowner who lose something that seems insignificant compared to what they already had. One lost sheep doesn't seem to matter all that much when you still have ninety-nine, or one lost coin out of a collection of ten. But in both cases, the love and compassion for what is lost outweighs the satisfaction of what is already there. Seems straightforward.

But the parable of the prodigal son offers so much nuance into understanding God's love. It's worth a whole chapter in this book. The Western teaching on this parable often misses some of the eastern nuance, and our appreciation over what Jesus was trying to teach is lost on some of us, the same way a non-musician cannot hear the notes not played in the jazz piece.

Although you've probably read it many times before, look at it with fresh eyes. Try to understand God's love as a benevolent King. "A man had two sons. The younger son told his father, 'I want my share of your estate now before you die.' So the father agreed to divide his wealth between his sons" (Luke 15:11).

Right away, something gets lost to the Western reader of this parable. It's common practice in our cultures to receive part of our inheritance before our parents die. In fact, many parents want to see their kids enjoy the wealth they have accumulated. So buying a house or giving money to help kids live beyond their means is natural.

Listeners of Jesus's parable would have had no such perspective. Multigenerational families lived together. Sons would work and live with their fathers, caring for them and their estates until the fathers' deaths. Then, the firstborn son would take the place as family head and lead the extended family of siblings and younger generations.

So this request made by the younger son is not only out of order, it's a complete sign of disrespect. He is asking for wealth that was not ever intended to be his. It would have belonged to the older brothers. Furthermore, he is asking for it while his father is still living. He is treating his father like he has passed on, taking wealth and leaving the family home. But the father shockingly agrees to give this great gift of money and independence to his young son, and the son goes to live his life as he pleases.

The parable is going much deeper than the lost coin or the lost sheep. This story is about a person who wants nothing to do with this father, who has generated wealth and notoriety of an estate. He represents the millions of people in our world who have decided that the life our heavenly Father has offered them is not one they want. They go their own way and live as if God doesn't even exist.

Jesus then describes what happens to this younger son. "He wasted all his money in wild living. About the time his money ran out, a great famine swept over the land and he began to starve. He persuaded a local farmer to hire him, and the man sent him into his fields to feed the pigs" (Luke 15:13–15).

Again, a basic understanding sees that trouble comes this younger son's way. He blows his money, and it's during a season of famine, so it's more difficult to survive. But the Jews understood famine as a direct sign of God's judgment on people. Those who were disobedient were punished with famine, while God protected His loved ones. From Joseph to Pharaoh to Jonah to Jezebel, the Jews understood all kinds of natural disasters as part of God's judgment on humankind. Those gathered to hear Jesus teach that day would have gotten to this part of the parable and agreed that God was judging the younger son because he turned his back. He deserved this famine.

Not only that, the contrast of being a son of a wealthy landowner or king was now living like a slave in a foreign land. It reinforced the idea to the Jews that God's blessing only existed when they stayed in the Father's land, with the chosen people of Israel.

The son is at his wit's end and decides to go home and beg for mercy, hoping to be treated as a slave in his father's home rather than be a slave far away. This man he was working for refused to give him even pig slop, and he would have known that his father was kind to his slaves and servants.

His return includes a fascinating description of how his father reacts. "So he returned home to his father. And while he was still

GOD'S LOVE IS LIKE…

a long way off, his father saw him coming. Filled with love and compassion, he ran to his son, embraced him and kissed him" (Luke 15:20).

In a Bible college years ago, there was a debate happening in a multicultural group of aspiring theologians about how to interpret this parable. It included European, Asian and African students. The Asian and African students, who understood tribalism much greater than the Europeans did, agreed that the fact that the father ran out to meet the son was a key piece to this story. In many cultures, the kind of disrespect shown to the father by the son was punishable only one way: death. *If you treat your father like he is dead, we treat you like you are dead.* And trying to come back is even a greater sign of disrespect, for he had quickly exhausted all the wealth the father had amassed over his entire life for his family. The fact that the father ran out to meet the son was in part because if the servants or extended family members had seen this prodigal son first, he would have never made it home. They would have avenged the disrespect shown to the father by killing the returning prodigal son.

It's also fascinating that the father is watching for the son. He knew that one day his son would return, and he already had a plan for him when he came.

> "Quick. Bring the finest robe in the house and put it on him. Get a ring for his finger and sandals for his feet. And kill the calf we have been fattening. We must celebrate with a feast, for this son of mine was dead and has now returned to life. He was lost, but now he is found." So the party began. (Luke 15:22–24)

The father acknowledges this concept of *being dead to me* in his welcome back. And although this son was willing to accept the position of a servant, he is immediately restored to the full privileges of a son.

The father kills the fatted calf and throws a party. For a calf to properly fatten for a feast takes months if not more than a year. The father lavishes years' worth of love on this returning son. This immediately sends the older brother into a rage. He probably said, "Seriously, Dad—you give half the wealth I deserve to him; he wastes it and disgraces you, ruining our family's reputation. And now when he comes back a complete failure, you invest more love and wealth into him. This is nuts. Who does that kind of thing?"

That's a great question. What kind of king has the kind of grace that allows people to choose to live outside the kingdom, with the king's blessing, and then can come back at any time and step right back in where they left off.

That's the love of our God. There is no person on earth who is not welcomed back into this family. God's grace is never earned. God's grace just is.

Humanity has spent the last two thousand years since Jesus's resurrection creating a religious system that creates insiders and outsiders. Those who live in a way that reflects the teachings of the Bible get to be insiders, and those who do not are outsiders. And sure, at times we celebrate when a person comes to faith, but they end up with "servant" status. We have boundaries for leadership or positions of honour, excluding those whose lives have not lived up to the standards of others. After all, it makes sense that honour should never be given; it should be earned.

That's what makes God love so amazing. His love is unmeasured to any of us. The world's system of hierarchy has no place in this kingdom. "There is no longer Jew or Gentile, slave or free, male and female. For you are all one in Christ Jesus" (Galatians 3:28).

Maybe at times you've felt as if you're an outsider in Christianity. You love God, but you can't seem to find your place in the church. Remember that people don't always get everything right, and the church is full of people. Jesus had to tell this parable on this day to a bunch of people who were trying to love God well. They needed to see that the older brother got it wrong. The best place for anyone who wants to follow God is to be in the church, making space for everyone to be sons and daughters of this benevolent king.

American author Rachel Held Evans says, "What makes the gospel offensive isn't who it keeps out but who it lets in."

God's love is truly unbelievable in this way.

CHAPTER 10
A Jealous Spouse Who Can't Stand to See Our Love and Attention Go toward Anything Else

I put these two chapters next to each other intentionally. I know I said in the introduction that it doesn't matter what order you read this book in, you can pick any chapter and read it on its own.

However, for this one, it's probably best to read chapter 8 before chapter 9. While this analogy is true, God's jealousy exists in complete contrast and perfect equilibrium with His grace. It's what makes understanding the entirety of God's love such a lifelong journey. We must make space for seemingly opposite expressions of God's love to coexist in harmony.

Which brings us to God's jealousy.

Paul regularly described the Church as the bride of Christ. He said that in the same way two individuals who join themselves in marriage become one, we become one with Christ as His bride. "As the Scriptures say, 'A man leaves his father and mother and is joined to his wife, and the two are united into one.' This is a great mystery, but it is an illustration of the way Christ and the church are one" (Ephesians 5:31–32).

It was the best human analogy for us to understand what becoming one with Christ looks like.

John talks about the bride of Christ in the book of Revelation. His vision of end time includes many references to the redeemed humans, who are resurrected with Jesus, being dressed and presented to Jesus as his bride. Again, it's a human depiction of what God wants to teach us about His love for us. We are as loved as a bride is on her wedding day, and as close as two people functioning as one can be. It's beautiful imagery.

But there is an expectation that comes with being a bride (or a husband, for that matter). When we choose to unite with each other, we also choose to focus all our love and attention on each other. We literally start to make decisions for the other's benefit instead of our own. We fight for their desires, not our own.

I often tell a joke at wedding ceremonies I am officiating. It's about the best fight they will ever have as a couple. The husband will come home one day and the lights will be low, and the wife will be sitting on the couch. She will pat the seat next to hear and inform the man that they need to have a little chat. No more terrifying words can be spoken to a husband than, "We need to have a chat."

All the ways you have failed as a man and a husband rush to your mind.

What did I break?

Did I not notice her haircut?

Have I been out too many nights this month?

Does she want to do another renovation project? Please, no more renovation projects! What if she's finally noticed that she's way out of my league and she's done with me?

So we brace ourselves and go sit on the couch. She'll let us know that she has noticed we are stressed, and that things are not going smoothly in the marriage. But not to worry, she knows the perfect way to fix it. She is sending you on a boys trip to watch sports, throw axes and be goofy. No kids, no responsibilities, just fun.

Suddenly the pressure is gone, and you as a husband are free to let her know that you love the idea, but you can't because you have booked her for a week away in Hawaii with her friends, and you are going to renovate the bathroom while she is gone to create his and hers spaces.

The fight is *for* each other, not *with* each other. Neither partner has to worry about caring for his or her own needs, because the other partner is doing that for both. In the end, both partners are loved well, and it's a better experience because your partner is doing it for you. That's when marriages work.

But almost every marriage that failed began when one of the partners started to turn his or her attention elsewhere. They started to notice another person. The got fixated on a hobby. They developed an addiction that took time and money that should have been invested in the marriage and put it into something self-centered.

This is how marriages fail. It starts fights *with* one another, as opposed to for. "I, the Lord your God, am a jealous God who will not tolerate your affection for any other gods" (Exodus 20:5).

Jealousy can often have a negative connotation, where we end up thinking it's about pettiness. We want something someone else has so we get jealous. Or we are so spoiled that the tiniest bit of attention paid elsewhere makes us angry and jealous. But since God self-describes part of His personality as jealous, it can't all be a bad thing.

God is trying to teach His followers that He desires to have our entire being focused on Him. He wants us to function as one, where we make decisions for our lives based solely out of love for Him. He wants us to trust that every need we will ever have will be taken care of if we focus everything we have on Him. In return, He promises that He'll care for our day-to-day needs, our greater worries and concerns and He'll even care for that eternal piece of us, our souls.

God will love us regardless of the choices we make and how much of our attention He gets. Nothing we do changes how God loves. But the relationship doesn't work so well when we get self-focused. When we start to make choices to provide for ourselves rather than letting God do it, we miss out on being one with Him. He is jealous for our love and attention because He knows how amazing a relationship we could have. He has focused everything on us, and now He is waiting for us to do so in return. He sacrificed all that He had—His very life—so that we would feel loved.

I think it's safe to describe God's heart as broken when he can't love Him back the way He loves us.

Jesus's interaction with Judas on the last night that He lived is a fascinating study. Jesus knew His ultimate purpose on earth was death, so it made no sense to stop Judas from doing what he was about to do. But Judas was a close friend of Jesus's. Few Bible scholars believe that when Jesus was choosing the twelve followers who would be His inner circle of disciples, He consciously knew it would be Judas who would betray Him. There were direct prophesies about the Son of God being betrayed, arrested and killed, and all were required to be fulfilled. But the combination of ways this could have taken place is immeasurable, and they don't all include one of the twelve being the facilitator to the treason. Most agree that Jesus chose Judas through leading the Holy Spirit. He invested every bit as much love and teaching into his life as He did with Simon, Thaddeus, Judas and the other disciples. The inner circle of Peter, James and John received perhaps more teaching and insight into Jesus's world, but Judas was by no means an outsider until he chose to make himself so at the end.

On the night they were celebrating Passover together, as they had done for the two years prior, Jesus's heart was heavy as He had seen what happened to Judas. He knew Judas had become a thief and that the plot to kill Him was on. "From that time on, Judas began looking for an opportunity to betray Jesus" (Matthew 26:16).

Yet in that upper room, Judas is still invited to participate in the intimacy of the Passover meal, and then Jesus freely welcomed Judas to go and betray Him. "Jesus responded, 'It is the one to whom I give the bread I dip in the bowl.' And when he had dipped it, he gave it to Judas, son of Simon Iscariot. When Judas had eaten the bread,

Satan entered into him. Then Jesus told him, 'Hurry and do what you're going to do'" (John 13:26–27).

God's jealousy is not self-serving. His jealousy is such that He wishes that a man like Judas, who had simply lost sight of God's plan in the name of religion, would have focused all his love and attention where it belonged, on God our Father.

That's the only way a marriage works well. Sure there are all kinds of negative ways that jealousy can play out when it's left in human hands. We can get petty and suspicious.

But as humans, we do that to all kinds of emotions that start as pure in the hands of God and end up corrupted when they are lived out on earth. His jealousy for our attention is to ensure that the marriage between Christ and His bride is healthy and thriving. His desire is that everyone whom He calls not only takes their seat around the table with Him but stays there for the entirety of the meal.

When Judas left to carry out his own mission, it broke the heart of the Jesus, who had such higher plans for Judas. A well-functioning marriage has a healthy jealousy for every bit of our partner's attention focused on us, so we can, in turn, love them back with the same intensity and devotion.

When you truly comprehend God's all-consuming love for you, it's easy to give it the all-consuming space it deserves in your life.

CHAPTER 11

An Adoptive Parent Who Chooses You for His Family, Yet Allows You to Set the Pace of Attachment

Full disclosure: this chapter is my favourite. At the very least, it's the example that, being an adoptive parent, I resonate with the most. The New Testament is full of teachings on how God chose people to be part of His family, even though it never seemed like they were destined to be part of the family. We've already discussed how Israel was indeed God's chosen people, but they were to be an example of what it looks like when God chooses people. So that when the right time came, God would extend his offer of becoming His sons and daughter to everyone in the world.

Paul wrote it this way to the Ephesian church: "God decided in advance to adopt us into his own family by bringing us to himself through Jesus Christ. This is what he wanted to do, and it gave him great pleasure" (Ephesians 1:5).

Ephesus is in modern-day Turkey, a good distance from Jerusalem and Israel. It was a church that had many Gentile believers, who up until a few years before had never considered that the Lord God wanted them in His family. This concept of adoption was quite new to them.

When my wife and I were in our late twenties, we had been married for six years. We were discussing the right time to have children. We got married very young and wanted to spend a few years establishing our careers and getting settled as adults and spouses before we threw kids into the mix.

That summer, Amanda travelled with a team from our church to China for a few weeks of missions. They were going to serve at a camp for kids with disabilities who had been orphaned or abandoned. China's strict child laws in 2008 restricted families to one child, and sadly, many children born with disabilities were abandoned to allow the couple to have another child. Amanda and her team spent two weeks as personal supports for kids as they participated in a summer camp called Bring Me Hope, allowing these kids a break from the group living quarters in which they normally resided.

During these weeks, God spoke clearly to her about how for many years, her job as an educator required her to be all these things to many kids: teacher, coach, encourager, advocate and more. But this was a new season of life, where God wanted her to become all things to one person by becoming a mom—through adoption!

Amanda and I had never discussed adoption before, so this came as a shock and surprise. When she returned home from the trip, she shared many reflections from her time in China but held back the piece about adoption. She had told God that if this were real, He would be responsible for telling me about it, not her!

The ultimatums we give God are sometimes funny.

The summer ended and fall began, with me being none the wiser of the deal Amanda had made with God. But in my personal prayer times, God began to speak to me about adoption, and Sonship into His family and the amazing miracle it was that I was chosen. There was even a time when I was studying these verses where I felt God speaking to me about adopting a child, and modelling the kind of love that I was learning about. However, since Amanda and I were still discussing having a baby the old-fashioned way, I thought it would be out of place.

One night on a long drive home, we were talking about what God had been speaking to us about, and I finally got the courage to share my reflections with Amanda. Her response left my jaw dropped: "God told me about adoption back in August, and I've been waiting for you to get around to hearing God as well!"

We researched the necessary steps and were accepted into a training program quite quickly. Given our age and professions and training, we were fast tracked through the process and approved as adoptive parents within a year. It was an exciting time, where we went through potential matches between children awaiting adoption with us. We spent nights and weekends dreaming and praying for the right child to be matched with us, so that we could start our family, like God started His.

But we quickly learned that adoption is little about the parents and mostly about the child. Regardless of our age, excitement or experience, the only factors that needed to be considered were the child's. Which family would be the best cultural, regional and experiential fit? These kids had been through loss and trauma, so every precaution was taken to select the exact right parents. Our waiting process went from months to a year to close to two years.

Our excitement turned to sadness and despair. While we had committed to God and the agency that we would stay focused on this adoption journey, it seemed to be turning into a dead end. Obviously, there was a much easier way to try to get this family going, so why were we enduring all this waiting and sadness? We determined to give it another month, pray about it, and maybe God would show us that it was time to move on.

One morning on her way to work, a worship song came on Amanda's playlist that spoke of solid trust in God and His paths for us. She clearly heard God say to her to just keep hope alive.

That day I received a call from our adoption worker for the first time in a long time. Apparently, there were two children that another agency had contacted her about that might be potential matches for us. One was a little younger who had experienced less trauma in her life and presently lived close to us.

The other had suffered serious losses in her young life. It would be a long journey for her to attach to a new family, so we might not want to pursue this relationship too hard.

Her name was Hope.

It's truly a remarkable experience when scripture becomes a real life experienced for you. Let's go back to that passage. "God decided in advance to adopt us into his own family by bringing us to himself through Jesus Christ. This is what he wanted to do, and it gave him great pleasure" (Ephesians 1:5).

"God decided in advance to adopt ~~us~~ HOPE into ~~his~~ our own family. He made it so plainly clear to us that we could simply not have missed what we were supposed to do.

~~... by bringing us to himself~~ We brought ourselves to her—meaning we would spend the next few months driving back and forth four to five hours a weekend to meet this little child. It was completely inconvenient and brought us through snowstorms on late nights, but all was worth it.

This is what ~~he~~ we wanted to do, and it gave ~~him~~ us great pleasure Looking back at our lives now, we would never have chosen anyone else. She's the perfect fit for our wild family: loud and hilarious like her dad, and a compassionate and caring leader like her mom.

And like God's love for us, our journey, as every parent's journey is more about our kids than us. We sacrifice comfort, resource, feelings and attention all toward them so they know they are loved.

God could have made it about Him, making us jump through hoops to join His family. Instead, He inconvenienced Himself, left his home and offered us the privilege of being called sons and daughters, even though we don't make it easy on him. "And I will be your Father, and you will be my sons and daughters, says the Lord Almighty" (2 Corinthians 6:18).

You and I are invited to be part of God's family, whether we feel like we deserve it. Some people have a family heritage of Christianity while others do not. Some people feel like they live life closely to how the Bible describes we should live while others definitely do not. Some go to church while others are out to Sunday brunch, like I was. And the scandalous thing about the love of God is that it is equally offered and extended to the whole lot of us, whether we feel we deserve it. Or whether we feel like someone else deserves it. We are all adopted into this family of God.

CONCLUSION

If you've not yet figured it out, God really loves you. You may not always feel it in every season of your life, and you may not perceive every interaction you have had with God as loving. But make no mistake—God has no other feeling directed toward you than love. His judgment is love, just as much as His forgiveness for you is love. His proud satisfaction for you as His child is love, yet His love helps Him see and have patience for the parts of you that are at times not worthy of love. And in one short little book, we can't come close to describing all aspects of God's love for His creation.

God's love is eternal, in that His love for you was the same at the time of creation, as it is for you while you are living, as it will be for all eternity.

God's love is equal for all people, so in the moments where we are praying for success for a job or to be selected for a role, God has as much love and care for the other candidates vying for what we want. And He indeed wants to give us all good gifts while we seem to be in competition with each other.

God's love is in totality, incomprehensible by mere humans, able to be experienced but never able to be known. We use analogies like the parables to describe it, but we can jump to wrong conclusions if we think we've done it justice. It is triune, making Father, Son and Spirit one, and expansive beyond all creation, covering over the multitude of sin we brought into this world. God's love can only be described in one word: Jesus.

Many people spend many years trying to figure out if they can find their space in church. It's a common experience to hear that people are OK with Jesus, just not the church so much. The church represents religion, and religion represents a great deal of hurt for people. Religion has for sure gotten it wrong over the years, but the great mission of the church is not to point people to church. It's to point people to Jesus. If you are focused on the broken people and processes of religion, you're missing the heart of religion. Religion is nothing more really than the flawed system, created by flawed people, to help us connect with a God who loves us perfectly. Every time I get together with people who are trying to understand God, just as I am, I recognize that I'm going to need to have patience and kindness and give just as many second chances as the God who loves me in all these different ways does—like a grandparent, a proud parent, a jealous spouse, a kindergarten teacher, a benevolent king, a caregiver, an honourable judge, a counselor, a love, an artist and an adoptive parent.

His love is all these things and more. If your eyes, ears and hearts are open, you'll probably uncover better analogies even than these to understand how much your Father loves you. God's love is like a lot of things, and I hope you experience His love in some new and creative way today.